HORSES
CHARTED DESIGNS

Celeste Plowden

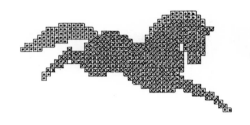

DOVER PUBLICATIONS, INC.
New York

Copyright © 1993 by Celeste Plowden.
All rights reserved under Pan American and International Copyright Conventions.

Published in Canada by General Publishing Company, Ltd., 30
Lesmill Road, Don Mills, Toronto, Ontario.
Published in the United Kingdom by Constable and Company,
Ltd., 3 The Lanchesters, 162–164 Fulham Palace Road, London W6
9ER.

Horses Charted Designs is a new work, first published by Dover
Publications, Inc., in 1993.

Library of Congress Cataloging-in-Publication Data

Plowden, Celeste.
    Horses charted designs / Celeste Plowden.
        p.   cm. — (Dover needlework series)
    ISBN 0-486-27578-7 (pbk.)
    1. Embroidery—Patterns.   2. Cross-stitch—Patterns.
3. Horses in art.   I. Title.   II. Series.
TT773.P55   1993
746.44'041—dc20
                                                            93-18960
                                                            CIP

Manufactured in the United States of America
Dover Publications, Inc., 31 East 2nd Street, Mineola, N.Y. 11501

Introduction

The partnership between horse and humans goes back centuries. Horses have been used to pull plows, wagons and coaches; they provide us with a fast and enjoyable means of transportation and they give us great pleasure in watching their beauty and grace as they race and jump. They also form a part of our fantasies—the unicorn and Pegasus are familiar figures in myths and legends. While children, particularly, are fascinated by horses, it is a fascination that never entirely disappears.

The designs in this collection show horses in all their guises—as worker, friend and fantasy. Here you will find various breeds and types of horses—trotters, a hunter, ponies, a Mustang, a Palomino and a Lippizaner; as well as horses at play, at work and at rest. Here too are fantasy horses—a carousel horse, a rocking horse, a winged horse and several unicorns. The designs vary from realistic portraits to elaborate borders in Baroque or Renaissance style, and all can be used to create samplers, pictures, pillows, placemats, tote bags and more.

Most of these designs were originally created for counted cross-stitch or needlepoint, but they are easily translated into other needlework techniques. Keep in mind that the finished piece will not be the same size as the charted design unless you are working on fabric or canvas with the same number of threads per inch as the chart has squares per inch. With knitting and crocheting, the size will vary according to the number of stitches per inch.

In cross-stitch, the background is normally left blank so that the fabric shows through. However, a number of these designs list a color number for the background. When this occurs, the motif was originally designed to be worked on a colored background. The color number can be used as a guide for selecting the fabric color for cross-stitch and the thread color for other forms of needlework. Naturally, of course the design can also be worked with any color background you wish.

COUNTED CROSS-STITCH

MATERIALS

1. **Needles.** A small blunt tapestry needle, No. 24 or No. 26.
2. **Fabric.** Evenweave linen, cotton, wool or synthetic fabrics all work well. The most popular fabrics are aida cloth, linen and hardanger cloth. Cotton aida is most commonly available in 18 threads-per-inch, 16 threads-per-inch, 14 threads-per-inch and 11 threads-per-inch (14-count is the most popular size). Evenweave linen comes in a variety of threads-per-inch. To work cross-stitch on linen involves a slightly different technique (see page 4). Thirty thread-per-inch linen will result in a stitch about the same size as 14-count aida. Hardanger cloth has 22 threads to the inch and is available in cotton or linen. The amount of fabric needed depends on the size of the cross-stitch design. To determine yardage, divide the number of stitches in the design by the thread-count of the fabric. For example: If a design 112 squares wide by 140 squares deep is worked on a 14-count fabric, divide 112 by 14 (= 8), and 140 by 14 (= 10). The design will measure 8″ × 10″. The same design worked on 22-count fabric measures about 5″ × 6½″. When cutting the fabric, be sure to allow at least 2″ of blank fabric all around the design for finishing.

3. **Threads and Yarns.** Six-strand embroidery floss, crewel wool, pearl cotton or metallic threads all work well for cross-stitch. DMC Embroidery Floss has been used to color-code the patterns in this volume.

4. **Embroidery Hoop.** A wooden or plastic 4″, 5″ or 6″ round or oval hoop with a screw-type tension adjuster works best for cross-stitch.

5. **Scissors.** A pair of sharp embroidery scissors is essential to all embroidery.

PREPARING TO WORK

To prevent raveling, either whip stitch or machine-stitch the outer edges of the fabric.

Locate the exact center of the chart. Establish the center of the fabric by folding it in half first vertically, then horizontally. The center stitch of the chart falls where the creases of the fabric meet. Mark the fabric center with a basting thread.

It is best to begin cross-stitch at the top of the design. To establish the top, count the squares up from the center of the chart, and the corresponding number of holes up from the center of the fabric.

Place the fabric tautly in the embroidery hoop, for tension makes it easier to push the needle through the holes without piercing the fibers. While working continue to retighten the fabric as necessary.

When working with multiple strands (such as embroidery floss) always separate (strand) the thread before beginning to stitch. This one small step allows for better coverage of the fabric. When you need more than one thread in the needle, use separate strands and do not double the thread. (For example: If you need four strands, use four separated strands.) Thread has a nap (just as fabrics do) and can be felt to be smoother in one direction than the other. Always work with the nap (the smooth side) pointing down.

For 14-count aida and 30-count linen, work with two strands of six-strand floss. For more texture, use more thread; for a flatter look, use less thread.

EMBROIDERY

To begin, fasten the thread with a waste knot and hold a short length of thread on the underside of the work, anchoring it with the first few stitches *(Diagram 1)*. When the thread end is securely in place, clip the knot.

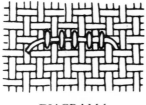

DIAGRAM 1
Reverse side of work

To stitch, push the needle up through a hole in the fabric, cross the thread intersection (or square) on a left-to-right diagonal *(Diagram 2)*. Half the stitch is now completed.

DIAGRAM 2

Next, cross back, right to left, forming an X *(Diagram 3)*.

DIAGRAM 3

DIAGRAM 4

Work all the same color stitches on one row, then cross back, completing the X's *(Diagram 4)*.

Some needleworkers prefer to cross each stitch as they come to it. This method also works, but be sure all of the top stitches are slanted in the same direction. Isolated stitches must be crossed as they are worked. Vertical stitches are crossed as shown in *Diagram 5*.

DIAGRAM 5

At the top, work horizontal rows of a single color, left to right. This method allows you to go from an unoccupied space to an occupied space (working from an empty hole to a filled one), making ruffling of the floss less likely. Holes are used more than once, and all stitches "hold hands" unless a space is indicated on the chart. Hold the work upright throughout (do not turn as with many needlepoint stitches).

When carrying the thread from one area to another, run the needle under a few stitches on the wrong side. Do not carry thread across an open expanse of fabric as it will be visible from the front when the project is completed.

To end a color, weave in and out of the underside of the stitches, making a scallop stitch or two for extra security *(Diagram 6)*. When possible, end in the same direction in which you were working, jumping up a row if necessary *(Diagram 7)*. This prevents holes caused by stitches being pulled in two directions. Trim the thread ends closely and do not leave any tails or knots as they will show through the fabric when the work is completed.

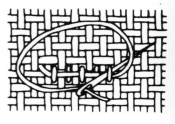

DIAGRAM 6
Reverse side of work

DIAGRAM 7
Reverse side of work

A number of other counted-thread stitches can be used in cross-stitch. Backstitch *(Diagram 8)* is used for outlines, face details and the like. It is worked from hole to hole, and may be stitched as a vertical, horizontal or diagonal line.

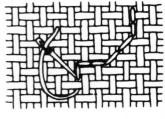

DIAGRAM 8

Straight stitch is worked from side to side over several threads *(Diagram 9)* and affords solid coverage.

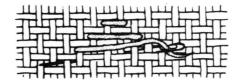

DIAGRAM 9

Embroidery on Linen. Working on linen requires a slightly different technique. While evenweave linen is remarkably regular, there are always a few thick or thin threads. To keep the stitches even, cross-stitch is worked over two threads in each direction *(Diagram 10)*.

DIAGRAM 10

As you are working over more threads, linen affords a greater variation in stitches. A half-stitch can slant in either direction and is uncrossed. A three-quarters stitch is shown in *Diagram 11*.

DIAGRAM 11

Diagram 12 shows the backstitch worked on linen.

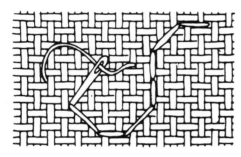

DIAGRAM 12

Embroidery on Gingham. Gingham and other checked fabrics can be used for cross-stitch. Using the fabric as a guide, work the stitches from corner to corner of each check.

Embroidery on Uneven-Weave Fabrics. If you wish to work cross-stitch on an uneven-weave fabric, baste a light-weight Penelope needlepoint canvas to the material. The design can then be stitched by working the cross-stitch over the double mesh of the canvas. When working in this manner, take care not to catch the threads of the canvas in the embroidery. After the cross-stitch is completed, remove the basting threads. With tweezers remove first the vertical threads, one strand at a time, of the needlepoint canvas, then the horizontal threads.

NEEDLEPOINT

One of the most common methods for working needlepoint is from a charted design. By simply viewing each square of a chart as a stitch on the canvas, the patterns quickly and easily translate from one technique to another.

MATERIALS

1. **Needles.** A blunt tapestry needle with a rounded tip and an elongated eye. The needle must clear the hole of the canvas without spreading the threads. For No. 10 canvas, a No. 18 needle works best.

2. **Canvas.** There are two distinct types of needlepoint canvas: single-mesh (mono canvas) and double-mesh (Penelope canvas). Single-mesh canvas, the more common of the two, is easier on the eyes as the spaces are slightly larger. Double-mesh canvas has two horizontal and two vertical threads forming each mesh. The latter is a very stable canvas on which the threads stay securely in place as the work progresses. Canvas is available in many sizes, from 5 mesh-per-inch to 18 mesh-per-inch, and even smaller. The number of mesh-per-inch will, of course, determine the dimensions of the finished needlepoint project. A 60 square × 120 square chart will measure 12″ × 24″ on 5 mesh-to-the-inch canvas, 5″ × 10″ on 12 mesh-to-the-inch canvas. The most common canvas size is 10 to the inch.

3. **Yarns.** Persian, crewel and tapestry yarns all work well on needlepoint canvas.

PREPARING TO WORK

Allow 1″ to 1½″ blank canvas all around. Bind the raw edges of the canvas with masking tape or machine-stitched double-fold bias tape.

There are few hard-and-fast rules on where to begin the design. It is best to complete the main motif, then fill in the background as the last step.

For any guidelines you wish to draw on the canvas, take care that your marking medium is waterproof. Nonsoluble inks, acrylic paints thinned with water so as not to clog the mesh, and waterproof felt-tip pens all work well. If unsure, experiment on a scrap of canvas.

When working with multiple strands (such as Persian yarn) always separate (strand) the yarn before beginning to stitch. This one small step allows for better coverage of the canvas. When you need more than one piece of yarn in the needle, use separate strands and do not double the yarn. For example: If you need two strands of 3-ply Persian yarn, use two separated strands. Yarn has a nap (just as fabrics do) and can be felt to be smoother in one direction than the other. Always work with the nap (the smooth side) pointing down.

For 5 mesh-to-the-canvas, use six strands of 3-ply yarn; for 10 mesh-to-the-inch canvas, use three strands of 3-ply yarn.

STITCHING

Cut yarn lengths 18″ long. Begin needlepoint by holding about 1″ of loose yarn on the wrong side of the work and working the first several stitches over the loose end to secure it. To end a piece of yarn, run it under several completed stitches on the wrong side of the work.

There are hundreds of needlepoint stitch variations, but tent stitch is universally considered to be *the* needlepoint stitch. The most familiar versions of tent stitch are half-cross stitch, continental stitch and basket-weave stitch.

Half-cross stitch *(Diagram 13)* is worked from left to right. The canvas is then turned around and the return row is again stitched from left to right. Holding the needle vertically, bring it to the front of the canvas

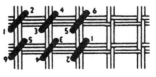

DIAGRAM 13

through the hole that will be the bottom of the first stitch. Keep the stitches loose for minimum distortion and good coverage. Half-cross stitch is best worked on a double-mesh canvas.

DIAGRAM 14

Continental stitch *(Diagram 14)* begins in the upper right-hand corner and is worked from right to left. The needle is slanted and always brought out a mesh ahead. The resulting stitch appears as a half-cross stitch on the front and as a slanting stitch on the back. When the row is complete, turn the canvas around to work the return row, continuing to stitch from right to left.

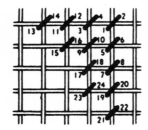

DIAGRAM 15

Basket-weave stitch *(Diagram 15)* begins in the upper right-hand corner with four continental stitches (two stitches worked horizontally across the top and two placed directly below the first stitch). Work diagonal rows, the first slanting up and across the canvas from right to left, and the next down and across from left to right. Moving down the canvas from left to right, the needle is in a vertical position; working in the opposite direction, the needle is horizontal. The rows interlock, creating a basket-weave pattern on the wrong side. If the stitch is not done properly, a faint ridge will show where the pattern was interrupted. On basket-weave stitch, always stop working in the middle of a row, rather than at the end, so that you will know in which direction you were working.

KNITTING

Charted designs can be worked into stockinette stitch as you are knitting, or they can be embroidered with duplicate stitch when the knitting is complete. For the former, wind the different colors of yarn on bobbins and work in the same manner as in Fair Isle knitting. A few quick Fair Isle tips: (1) Always bring up the new color yarn from under the dropped color to prevent holes. (2) Carry the color not in use loosely across the wrong side of the work, but not more than three or four stitches without twisting the yarns. If a color is not in use for more than seven or eight stitches, it is usually best to drop that color yarn and rejoin a new bobbin when the color is again needed.

CROCHET

There are a number of ways in which charts can be used for crochet. Among them are:

SINGLE CROCHET

Single crochet is often seen worked in multiple colors. When changing colors, always pick up the new color for the last yarn-over of the old color. The color not in use can be carried loosely across the back of the work for a few stitches, or you can work the single crochet over the unused color. The latter method makes for a neater appearance on the wrong side, but sometimes the old color peeks through the stitches. This method can also be applied to half-double crochet and double crochet, but keep in mind that the longer stitches will distort the design.

FILET CROCHET

This technique is nearly always worked from charts and uses only one color thread. The result is a solid-color piece with the design filled in and the background left as an open mesh. Care must be taken in selecting the design, as the longer stitch causes distortion.

AFGHAN CROCHET

The most common method here is cross-stitch worked over the afghan stitch. Complete the afghan crochet project. Then, following the chart for color placement, work cross-stitch over the squares of crochet.

OTHER CHARTED METHODS

Latch hook, Assisi embroidery, beading, cross-stitch on needlepoint canvas (a European favorite) and lace net embroidery are among the other needlework methods worked from charts.

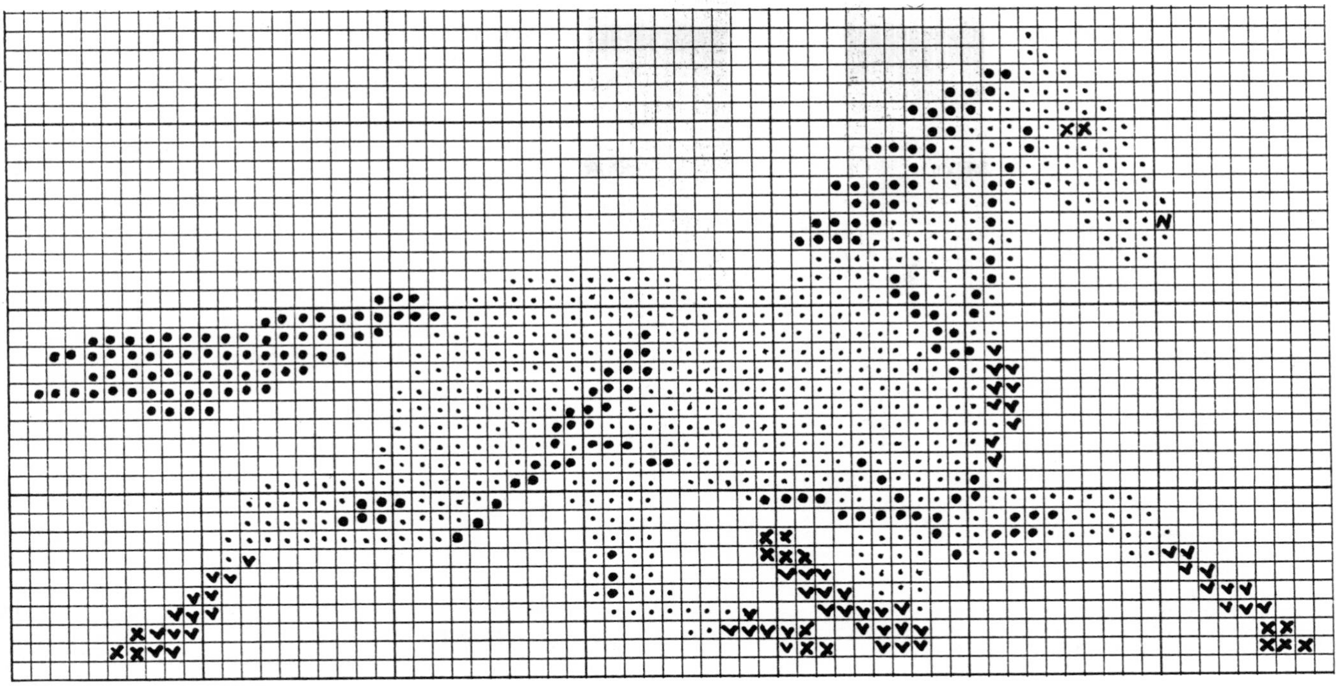

▲ Chestnut Trotter

67 stitches by 34 stitches

	DMC #	
V		white
·	300	very dark mahogany
X	310	black
●	434	light brown
N	899	medium rose

▼ Gray Trotter

67 stitches by 34 stitches

	DMC #	
·		white
X	310	black
●	318	light steel gray
V	899	medium rose

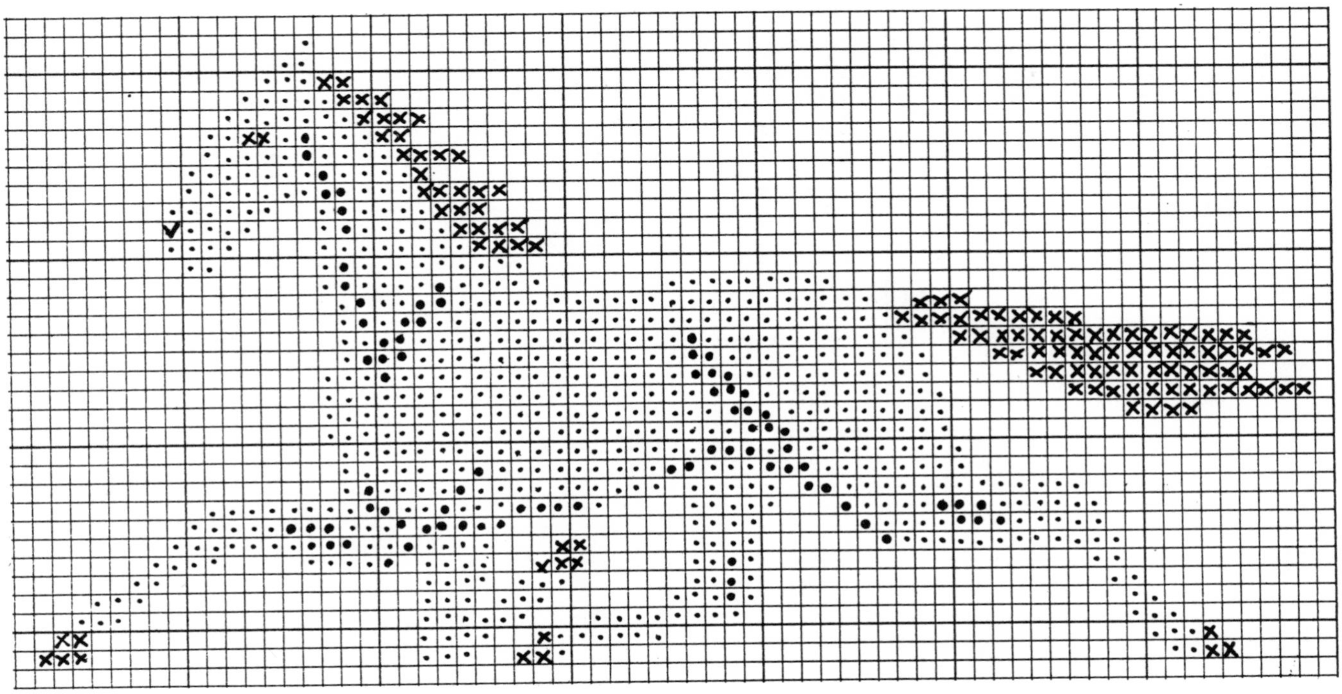

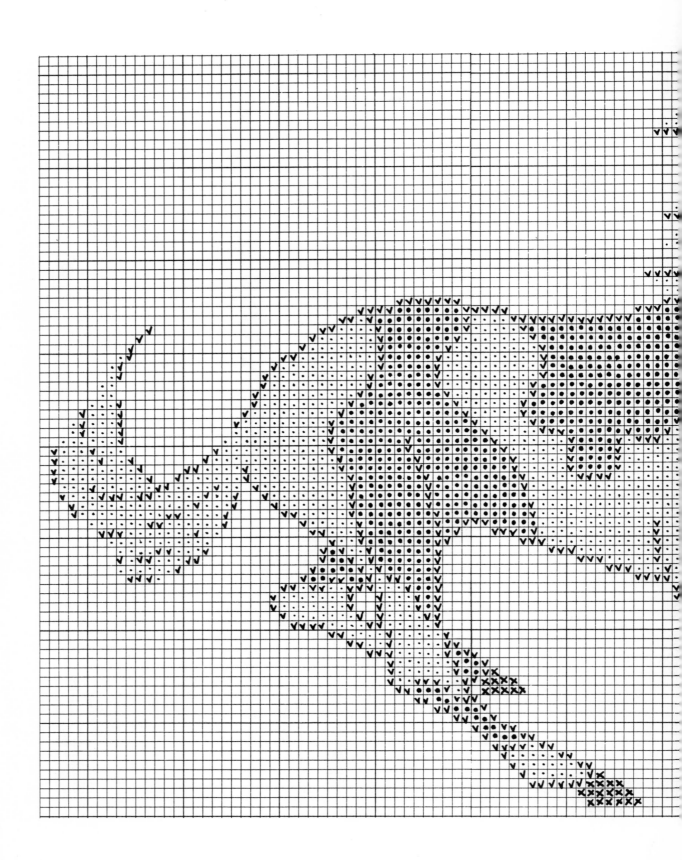

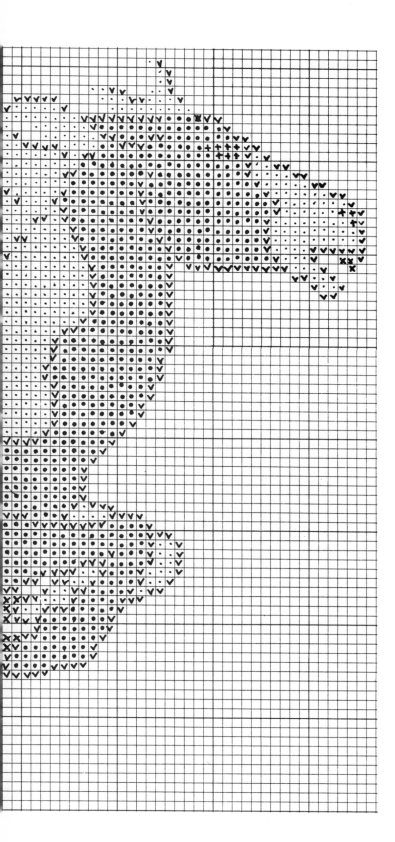

Skewbald Mustang

110 stitches by 80 stitches

	DMC #	
☒		white
⊙	729	medium old gold
·	746	off white
⊞	838	very dark beige brown
☑	3045	dark yellow beige
☐ {	221	very dark pinkish brown (background)
	797	royal blue (background)
	937	medium avocado green (background)

If desired, use one of the background colors suggested above.

Horses at Play

140 stitches by 95 stitches

DMC #

Ⅼ	208	very dark lavender
☒	310	black
⊟	320	medium pistachio green
Ⓝ	322	dark marine blue
Ⅱ	351	coral
◣	712	cream
∴	727	very light topaz
⊞	738	very light tan
●	801	dark coffee brown
Ⅴ	987	medium forest green
☐	800	pale Delft blue (background)

If desired, use the background color suggested above.

Medieval Scene for Sampler

140 stitches by 80 stitches

BACK-STITCH	CROSS-STITCH	DMC #	
	●		white
	☑	221	very dark pinkish brown
	◪	223	medium pinkish brown
	⫿	300	very dark mahogany
	☒	310	black
	Ⓝ	321	Christmas red
	③	327	dark gray violet
	Ⓕ	340	medium lilac

	BACK-STITCH	CROSS-STITCH	DMC #	
		田	500	very dark blue green
		Λ	502	blue green
		⊡	729	medium old gold
		L	739	fawn beige
		II	815	medium garnet red
	——	b	839	dark beige brown
		田	840	medium beige brown
		⊡	948	very light peach

Rainbow Horses

each repeat, 51 stitches by 23 stitches

Bright Colors

	DMC #	
◲	307	lemon yellow
◪	552	dark violet
⛉	608	bright orange
⊙	666	bright Christmas red
·	798	dark Delft blue
⊠	911	medium emerald green

Pastel Colors

	DMC #	
⛝	210	medium lavender
⛛	353	peach
⛝	368	light pistachio green
◲	744	medium yellow
●	776	medium pink
·	3325	baby blue

15

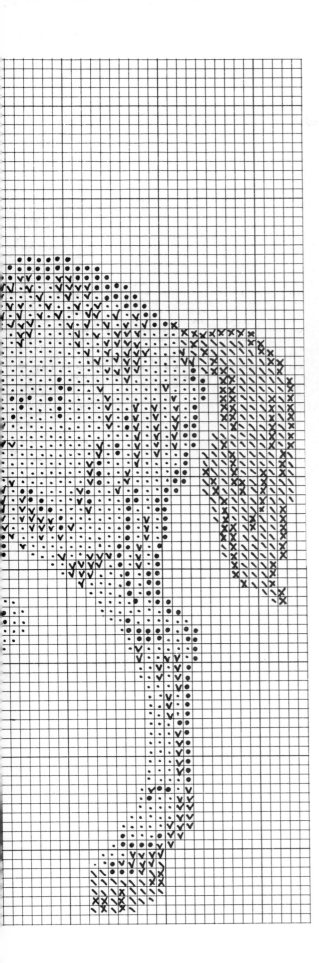

Palomino

98 stitches by 91 stitches

	DMC #	
·	676	light old gold
V	677	very light old gold
●	729	medium old gold
X	739	fawn beige
⟍	746	off-white
■	801	dark coffee brown

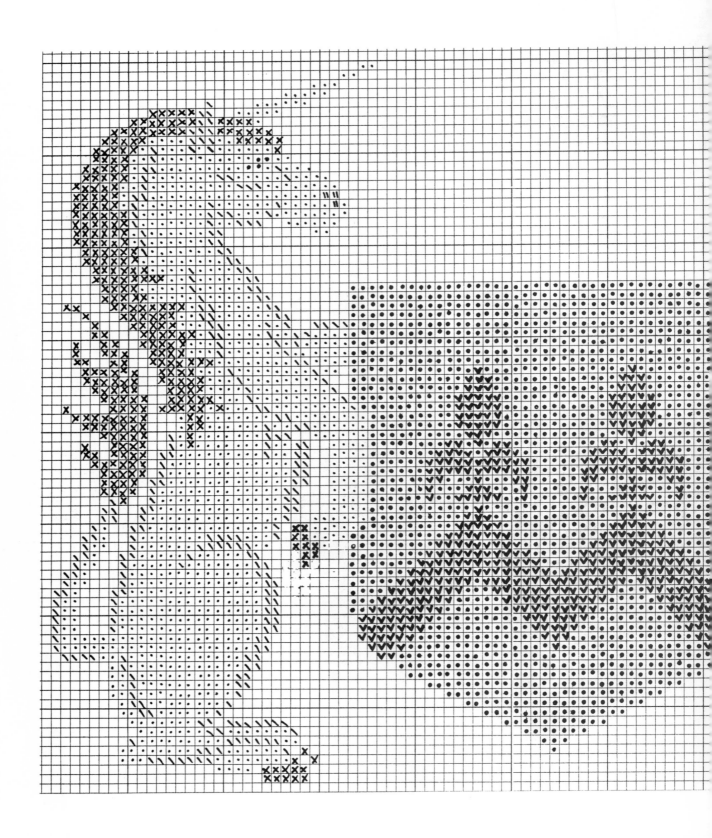

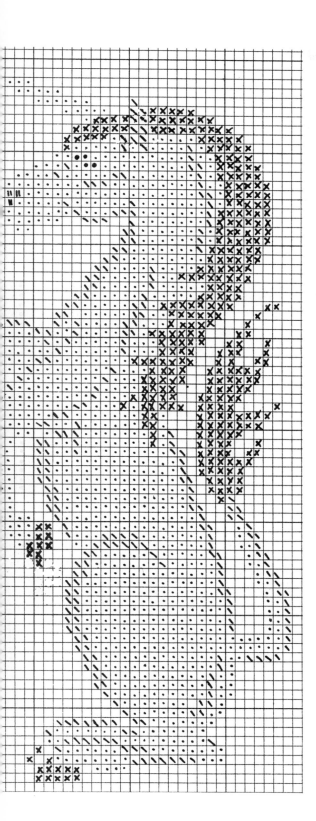

Heraldic Unicorns

105 stitches by 78 stitches

DMC #

·		white
Ⅲ	310	black
Ⅴ	725	topaz
●	797	royal blue
＼	822	light beige gray
☒	841	light beige brown
☐	815	medium garnet red (background)

If desired, use background color suggested above.

Allover Pattern
each repeat, 33 stitches by 24 stitches

Use any contrasting colors, or various colors.

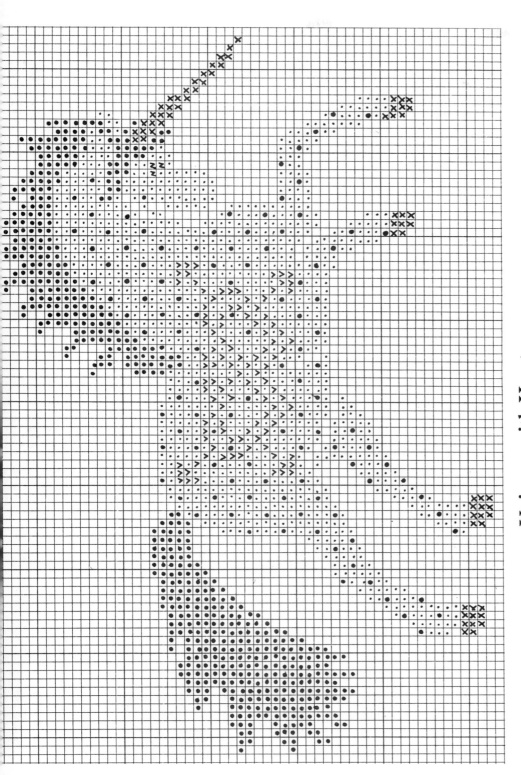

Unicorn with Hearts

86 stitches by 58 stitches

DMC #

·		white
●	310	black
V	321	Christmas red
N	601	dark cranberry
X	725	topaz
☐	815	medium garnet red (background)

If desired, use background color suggested above.

Garden on the Hilltop

140 stitches by 99 stitches

	DMC #	
⊡		ecru
■	209	dark lavender
4	351	coral
⊙	367	dark pistachio green
ΙΙ	498	dark Christmas red
V	727	very light topaz
X	791	very dark cornflower blue
⦂•	792	dark cornflower blue
L	822	light beige gray
P	838	very dark beige brown
I	950	light cocoa brown
3	951	light apricot
∧	961	dark dusty pink
⊞	3023	light brown gray
◺	3046	medium yellow beige
☐	793	medium cornflower blue (background)

If desired, use background color suggested above.

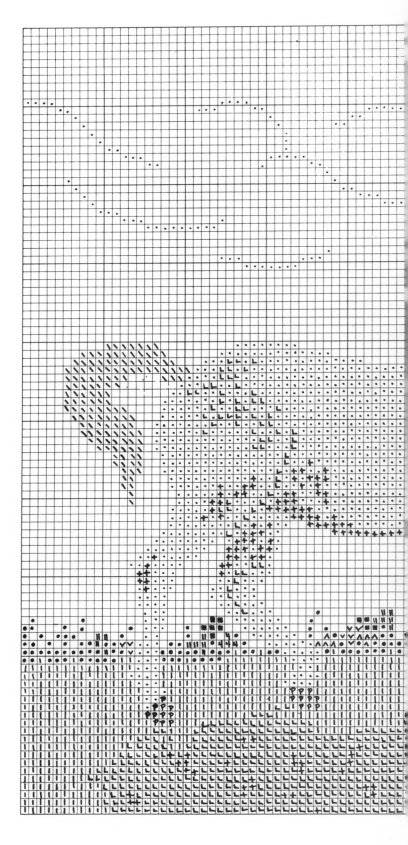

22

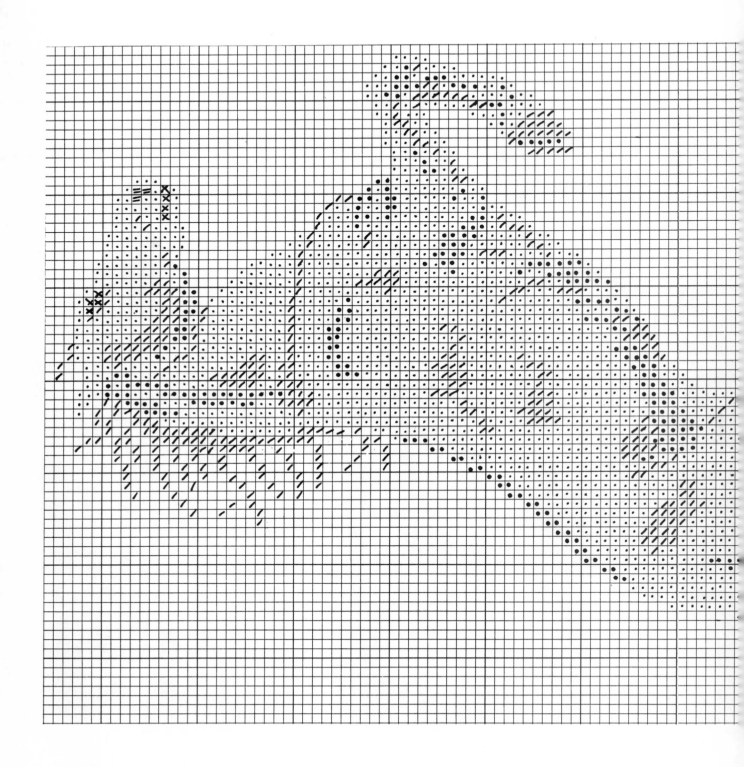

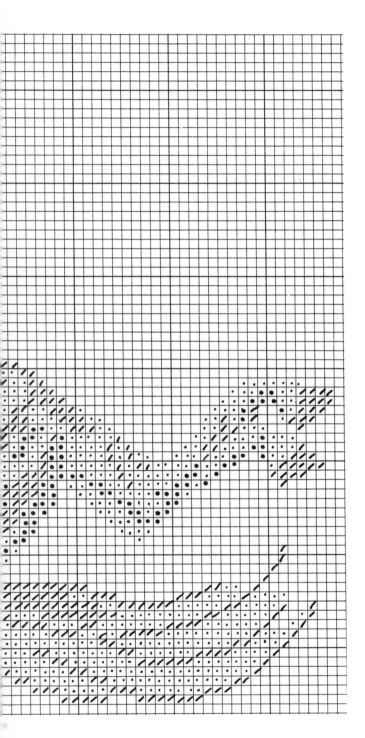

Lippizaner Stallion

71 stitches by 112 stitches

DMC #

⊡		white
⠿	224	light pinkish brown
◉	644	light beige gray
◪	822	light beige gray
☒	840	medium beige brown
☐	⎰ 502	blue green (background)
	⎱ 930	dark antique blue (background)
	3685	dark mauve (background)

If desired, use one of the background colors suggested above.

Appaloosa in Pink

64 stitches by 61 stitches

DMC #

⊙	309	deep rose
⊠	322	dark marine blue
☑	766	deep rose
⊡	899	medium rose

Rocking Horse

61 stitches by 46 stitches

	DMC #	
☒	309	deep rose
⊙	518	light Wedgwood blue
◿	519	sky blue
☑	726	light topaz
⊡	899	medium rose

Outline rockers in backstitch using 519 sky blue.

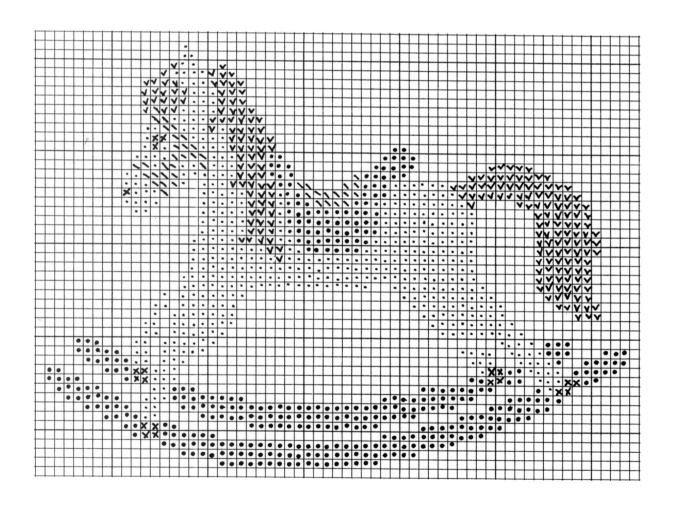

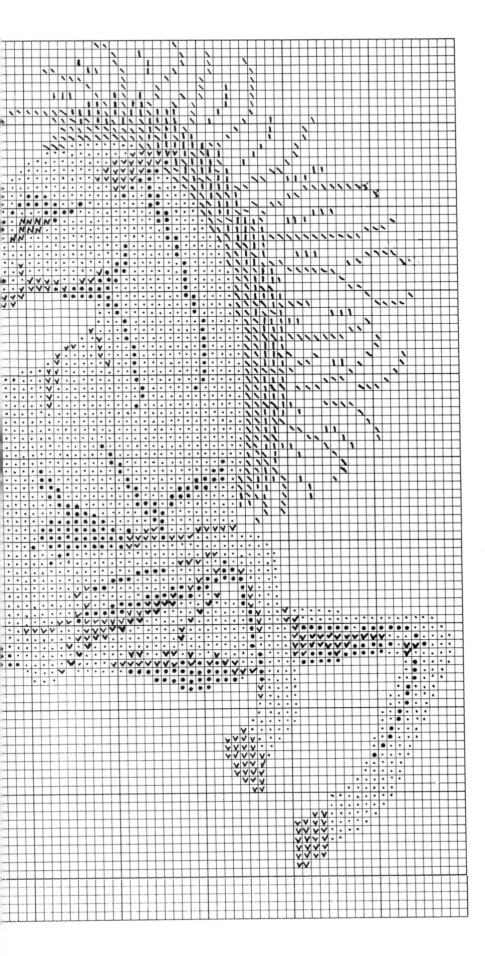

Fantasy Horse

129 stitches by 105 stitches

	DMC #	
◺	796	dark royal blue
Ⅱ	798	dark Delft blue
·	799	medium Delft blue
⬤	800	pale Delft blue
☑	823	dark navy blue
N	3685	dark mauve

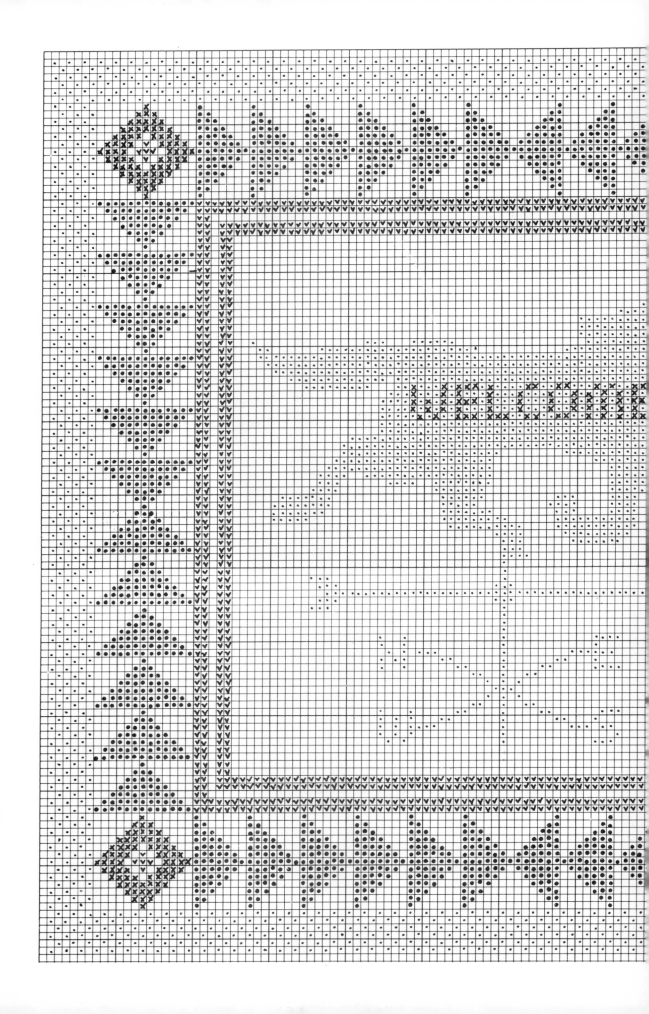

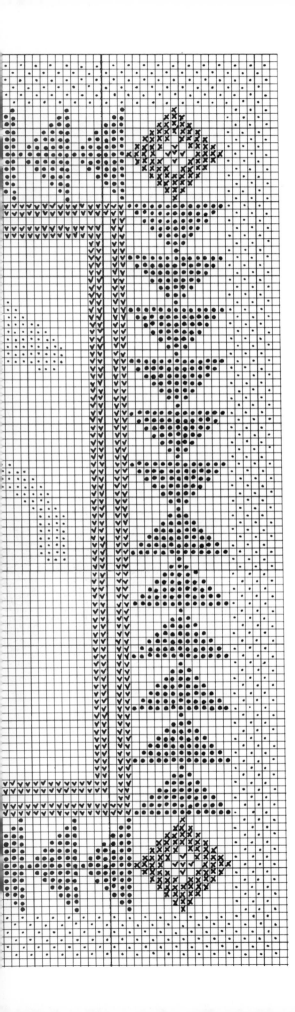

Weather Vane Sampler

121 stitches by 121 stitches

	DMC #	
☑	402	very light mahogany
·	930	dark antique blue
●	931	medium antique blue
☒	3328	medium dark salmon

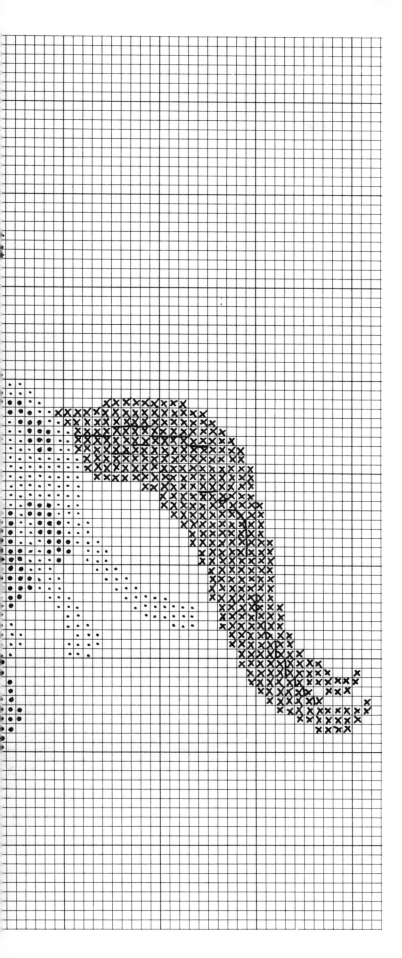

Medieval Knight on Horseback
117 stitches by 94 stitches

BACK-STITCH	CROSS-STITCH	DMC #	
	●	310	black
	L	318	light steel gray
	V	321	Christmas red
	L	413	dark pewter gray
	X	414	dark steel gray
	4	552	dark violet
	·	603	cranberry
	⊞	725	topaz
	3	798	dark Delft blue
	II	932	light antique blue

Icelandic Ponies

100 stitches by 92 stitches

DMC #

⊡		white
⊞	223	medium pinkish brown
Ⓝ	224	light pinkish brown
⊡	676	light old gold
Ⓥ	677	very light old gold
☒	761	light salmon
Ⓑ	841	light beige brown
⊙	842	very light beige brown
Ⓘ	932	light antique blue
◥	3348	light yellow green
☐	336	navy blue (background)

If desired, use background color suggested above.

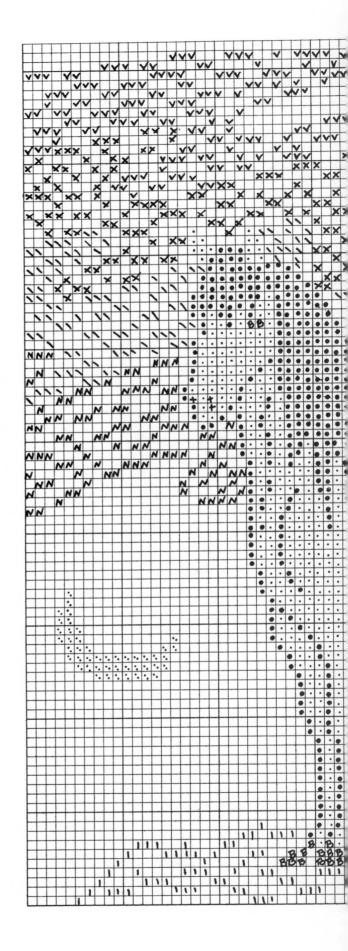

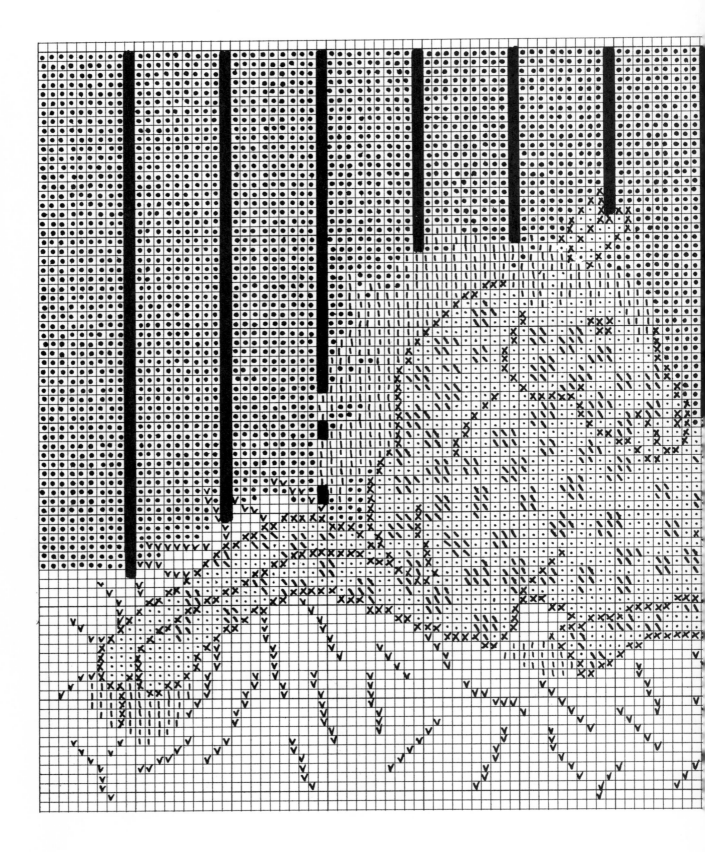

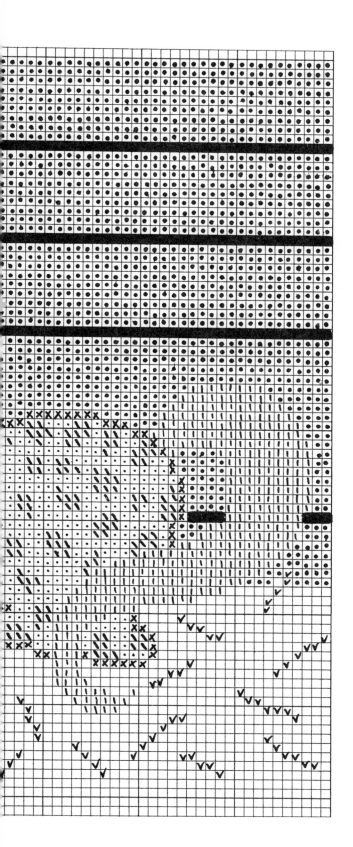

In the Stall

110 stitches by 81 stitches

DMC #

⊡		white
⬤	347	dark salmon
☒	413	dark pewter gray
Ⅱ	414	dark steel gray
◺	762	very light pearl gray
☑	3045	dark yellow beige
■	3328	medium dark salmon
☐	729	medium old gold (background)

If desired, use background color suggested above.

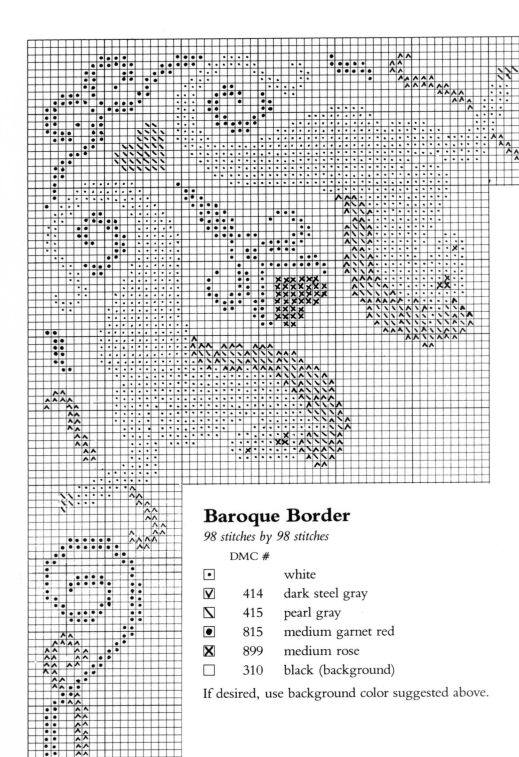

Baroque Border

98 stitches by 98 stitches

	DMC #	
•		white
⩔	414	dark steel gray
◸	415	pearl gray
●	815	medium garnet red
✖	899	medium rose
☐	310	black (background)

If desired, use background color suggested above.

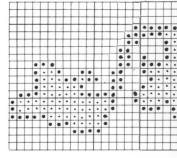

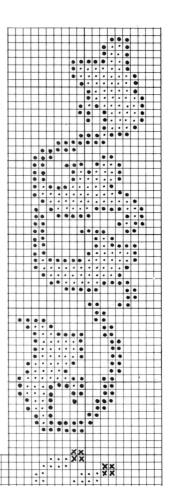

Renaissance Border

115 stitches by 115 stitches

	DMC #	
V	318	light steel gray
X	413	dark pewter gray
•	676	light old gold
◉	729	medium old gold
☐	815	medium garnet red (background)

If desired, use background color suggested above.

Horses and Sleigh

94 stitches by 14 stitches

Use color desired.

Classical Motif

129 stitches by 119 stitches

DMC #

- ● 310 black
- ☐ 355 very dark terra-cotta (background)

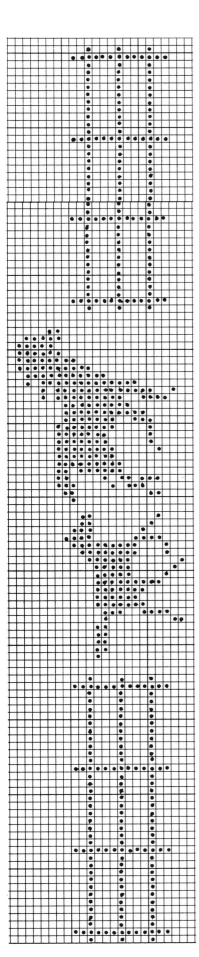

Fences
121 stitches by 22 stitches

Use color desired.

Coach
118 stitches by 22 stitches

Use color desired.

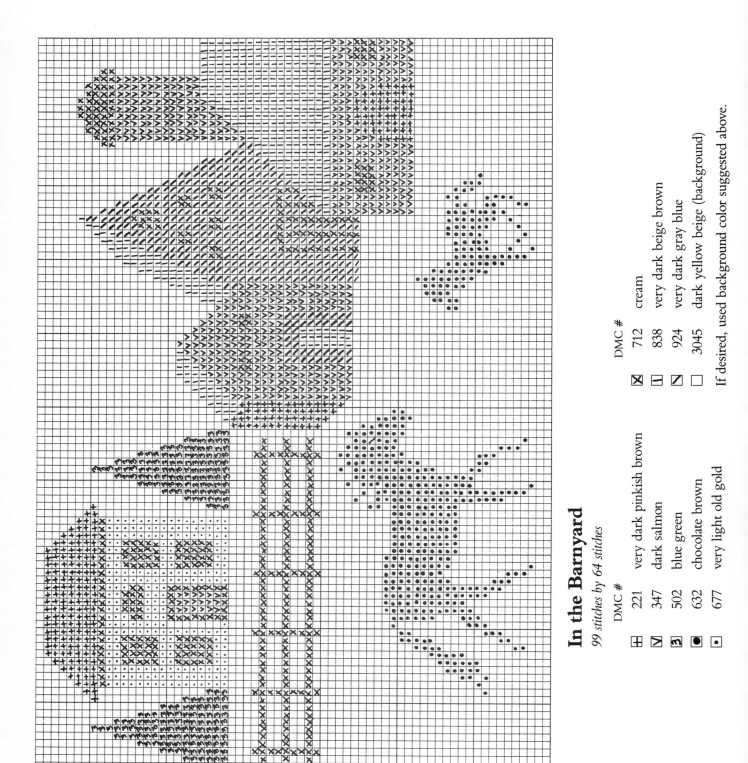

In the Barnyard

99 stitches by 64 stitches

DMC #

⊞	221	very dark pinkish brown
⋁	347	dark salmon
▨	502	blue green
⬤	632	chocolate brown
·	677	very light old gold

DMC #

⊠	712	cream
⊟	838	very dark beige brown
⧄	924	very dark gray blue
☐	3045	dark yellow beige (background)

If desired, used background color suggested above.

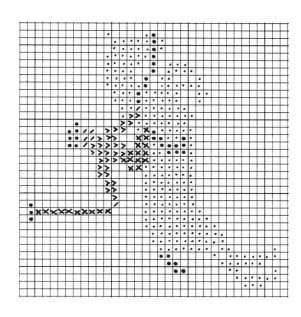

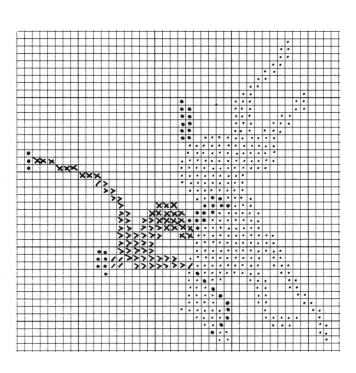

Polo

left, 41 stitches by 40 stitches
right, 35 stitches by 33 stitches

DMC #

·	300	very dark mahogany
●	310	black
✔	321 or 796	Christmas red / dark royal blue
✖	738	very light tan
◢	951	light apricot

Baroque Horse in Foliage

105 stitches by 96 stitches

	DMC #	
☑		white
฿	310	black
⊡	320	medium pistachio green
◉	368	light pistachio green
𝕀	815	medium garnet red
⊞	822	light beige gray
☒	890	ultra dark pistachio
ℕ	902	very dark garnet red
◺	3347	medium yellow green
☐	3685	dark mauve (background)

If desired, use background color suggested above.

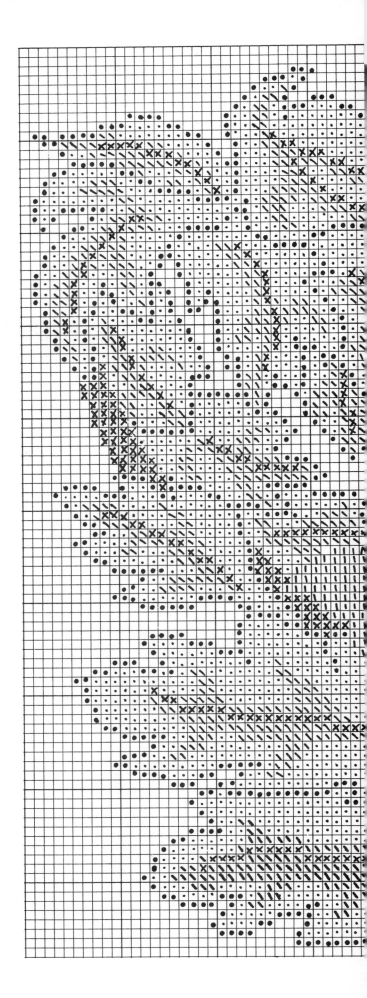

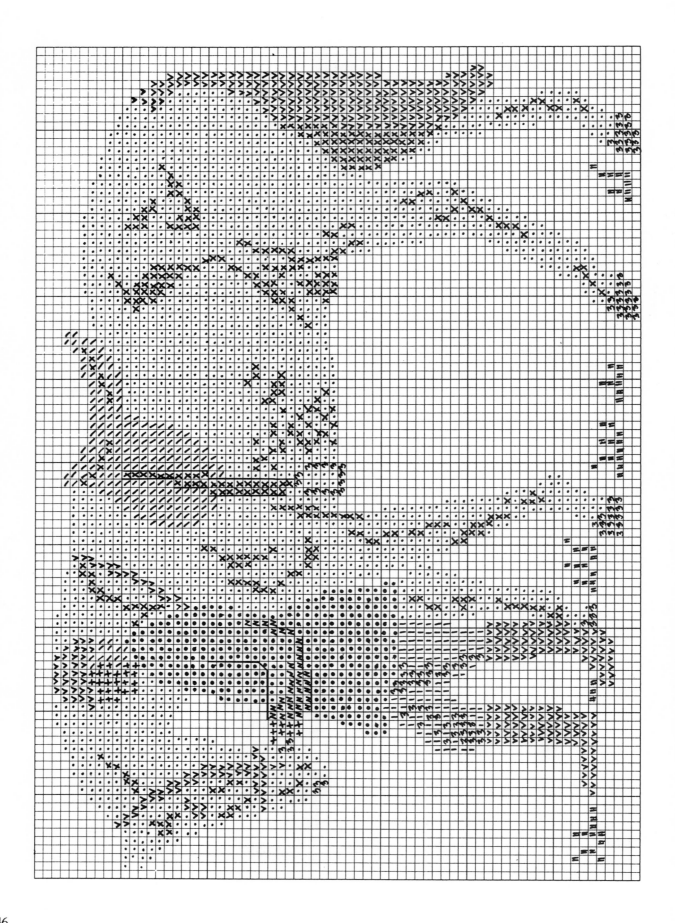